Your Path

From
Secret
to
Success

7-week Quick-Start Sales Guide

By
Jackie Simmons

ALSO BY JACKIE SIMMONS

Overcoming Mediocrity: Resilient Women (Volume 5)
https://amzn.to/2CiRUeV

Life Boosts: Strategies, Tactics, and Ideas to Boost Your Wealth, Health, and More!

The Game Changer (Volume 3)
https://amzn.to/2Cm3uGu

Make It A Great Day: The Choice Is Yours

Unscripted: How Women Thrive in Life, Business, and Relationships
https://amzn.to/2spsh80

Your Amazing Itty Bitty® Business Experts Compilation Book

Your Path

From Secret to Success

7-week Quick-Start Sales Guide

Spotlight Pubishing™
Goodyear, AZ

© 2018 Copyright Jackie Simmons
Jackie Simmons
Your Path From Secret to Success: 7-week Quick-Start Sales Guide

Published in the USA by MBK Enterprises, LLC | Spotlight Publishing, Goodyear, AZ

ISBN: ISBN-13: 978-1-953806-19-2

All rights reserved. No part of this book may be reproduced or transmitted in any form or by any means, electronic or mechanical, including photocopying, recording, or by any information storage and retrieval system, (electronic, mechanical, photocopying, recording or otherwise) without the prior written permission of the publisher. This book is sold subject to the condition that it shall not, by way of trade or otherwise, be lent, resold, hired out, or otherwise circulated without the publisher's prior consent in any form of binding or cover other than that in which it is published and without a similar condition, including this condition being imposed on the subsequent purchaser.

Editor: Mary Lou Stark   www.BookEnchantress.com
Cover: Celia Triplett   www.innerfiregraphicdesign.com
Interior Layout: www.speedreadamerica.com

Your Path From Secret to Success: 7-week Quick-Start Sales Guide

Jackie Simmons

Email: Jackie@SuccessJourneyAcademy.com
Website: www.SuccesJourneyAcademy.com

Table of Contents

PREFACE ii

Welcome to the 7-week Quick-Start Sales Guide! iv

Make More Money Loving What You Do vi

How to Use This Book: vi

Lessons I had to Learn: vii

Lesson 1 – *RELAX* – It's Just An "Elephant" 3

Lesson 2: – LISTEN – It's All About "Them," Their "Mess," Their "Message," and Their "Why" – Except When It Isn't… 17

Lesson 3: – *SERVE* – It's About Helping Them HIRE You! 29

Lesson 4 – ACT – "Leap And The Net Will Appear*"... Eventually 43

Lesson 5: – CREATE – You Only Get One Story In This Lifetime... The One That You Create. 59

Lesson 6: – SHARE – It's The Best Way to Help Them 75

Lesson 7: – ACHIEVE – Growth Is Continuous. 89

Achieve – Measure – Repeat 105

About the Author 109

Dedication

For Mark Walzer whose unconditional love and support made the journey to becoming an author possible and for Wendy Keilin whose limitless patience and excellent wordsmithing skills made the original of this book happen faster than I could have ever dreamed.

PREFACE

Ever wish you had an accelerator for your business? Or, that there was a way to take the "brakes off" so you could grow faster? Ever feel like you and your business are invisible?

I did!

I took training, attended seminars and networking events, I volunteered and promoted non-profits and other people's businesses, all in the belief that I was "growing" my business by growing my network. I "Linked," "Friended" and "Liked" and while I was fairly popular, I was often "just over broke." I considered going back into corporate and working a "real job." At least with a job, I wouldn't be dealing with the entrepreneurial schedule insanity.

Then, I made a decision that started a crazy rocket-ride of accelerated action and growth and chaos, and I was propelled from Secret to Success in 7 months! Just to be clear, I did not start my business and zoom to "Success" in 7 months. I had been in "business" for over 30 years. I put the quotes around "business" because "businesses" are supposed to make money, and I had a challenged track record in that regard. I had lived out a money story that was far from prosperous.

For the money story to change, I knew I needed to be seen as an expert in my field and recognized for bringing incredible value to my clients. I would build up a few clients, lose a few clients, build up a small program and then stop it when the seats didn't fill.

If this is your story, then this book is for you.

Do you know what is stopping you from speaking up and standing out?

I didn't.

Others tried to point me in the right direction, yet I seemed incapable of performing consistent actions or sustaining revenue. The fact that I couldn't see for myself what was in the way led me to conclude that despite all the training, mentoring, and inner work I had done, I was still dealing with mental and emotional blocks. Those blocks acted like an "Elephant in the Room" that sat on my phone, so I couldn't make sales calls and distracted me so that I couldn't focus and finish projects.

My "Elephants" kept me distracted, frustrated, and overwhelmed, making success seem impossible. I searched and studied – sometimes desperately seeking ways to remove, or at least "tame" them! Along the way, I discovered an attitude that changed the blocks into rocket fuel that propelled me into focused actions and accelerated growth.

Imagine being free from the all too familiar anxiety of not reaching out to ideal clients who actually want and need you. Imagine confidently going for the high-end clients that you know you are ready to serve. When I reviewed my 7-month rocket-ride, there were obvious shifts in how I did things.

What I learned and put into action is now this 7-week Quick-Start Guide. Why only 7 weeks? Because I don't think anyone else should have to wait 30 years to become the complete success they were always meant to be.

Welcome to the 7-week Quick-Start Sales Guide!

This is the fast path to doing things a bit differently (which is the only way to get different results).

I applaud your insight and bravery.

To get the most out of this Guide — here are the guidelines, a.k.a., rules.

The Rules of the Game:

No skipping Lessons, and keep going, even when (especially when) you feel stuck or confused!

No matter what your logical brain says, doing the Lessons, in order, is the fastest path to success.

Doing the lessons out of order will only slow you down.

I repeat: Doing the lessons out of order will only slow you down.

You can trust me on this; I had the Lessons mixed up for a very long time. During most of my business life, I jumped straight into action (Lesson 4). After all, I was smart; I could figure it out. And usually, I did, eventually.

Eventually... after long stretches of being broke!

The Lessons may seem to be devoid of any logical order – I get that. They're not. The order is very purposeful, and it works.

Based on my experience and those of my clients, the fastest way to shift from Secret to Success is to do the Lessons, in order, one at a time. I will continue to remind you, in the hopes of keeping you from jumping ahead and wasting time the way I did. That's it; there's only the 1 Rule.

The full explanation of how and why this sequence works is explored in the Lessons themselves. Get ready. Success will come faster now, and each week, you will be much further down the road!

Make More Money Loving What You Do

How to Use This Book:

Read each week's story and do any beginning exercises. Read the entire activity for each day and make time to complete it and whatever practice may be needed. It might be easier to do the reading in the morning, practice during the day, and then jot down your experiences in the evening.

Reread the stories as often as you like, repeat the exercises and applications multiple times during the day – just remember – no reading ahead. Reading ahead will only slow down your progress.

You can do the exercises right in the book or use a separate journal. If you use a journal, what we've found is that keeping the journal and book together is a habit worth forming...

NOTE: I highly recommend that you wait to design, order, or reorder business cards or other marketing materials until after you have completed the guide.

Your message may change (mine did).

Lessons I had to Learn:

1. It's not about me; there is nothing wrong with me.
   It's about staying present. – *RELAX* –

2. It's not about my "mess," my "message" or my "why."
   It's about theirs. – *LISTEN* –

3. It's not about "proving my value" or "selling."
   It's about helping. – *SERVE* –

4. It's not about getting it right.
   It's about getting it done. – *ACT* –

5. It's not about having a "shame-full" story.
   It's about not letting the fear of being judged for it, make it the only story I live. – *CREATE* –

6. It's not about being seen as perfect.
   It's about being seen as real and relatable. – *SHARE* –

7. It's not about arriving.
   It's about growing. – *ACHIEVE* –

LESSONS

Your Path From Secret to Success

Lesson 1
– *RELAX* –
It's Just An "Elephant"

The Elephant in the Room:

"Relaxing" is not something we do well in this current age. We were given multi-faceted, completely functional emotional awareness systems that were elegantly designed for our mutual ancestor – the caveman. The system worked perfectly in the caveman's world. The lightning speed of the stress response allowed our ancestors to survive.

Today, this same system is not working for us as well. We won't dive into the details of your brain in this book; it's only important to know that there is nothing wrong with you.

They just forgot to give you the owner's guide/instruction manual for your life. Without the instruction manual, this elegantly simple system inhibits our ability to take risks, tackle challenges, or try something new.

Don't laugh – the cure for this whole stress response mess is super simple.

Breathe.

Yup, that's it. It really is that simple. I told you not to laugh.

Your Path From Secret to Success

I'll prove it to you. Stop right now and rate your overall body tension. On a scale of 1 – 10, where 10 is completely uptight – what's your number?

Write it here: _____

Now, slowly fill your lungs with air, pause, and then release the air even more slowly. Breathe in again. Notice the air flowing into your body. Notice the way your body releases the air effortlessly.

Now notice the movement of your mind, as you consciously breathe in, not just air, but confidence. And, breathe out, releasing anything that is not that.

Breathe in again – filling your mind with confidence. Now breathe out, releasing anything that is not that.

Check your body again, using the same scale: 1-10, where 10 is completely uptight. What's your number now?

Write it here: _____

Notice the difference in how you feel. Take a minute and jot down, here or in your notebook, whatever's on your mind now that your body's more relaxed.

_____
_____
_____
_____
_____

Lesson 1: Day 1

– RELAX –

It's not about you, there is nothing wrong with you. It's about staying present.

Applying the Lesson:

For today and every day, practice taking 3 deep, slow breaths every hour during the day. Set the alarm on your phone. When it goes off, pause and take three deep, slow breaths. Another great place to practice is whenever you are at a red traffic light.

Finally, do this practice before you pick up your phone – either to make or answer a call. Do this especially when the caller is a "breath-stealer." You know, one of those people who when you see their Caller ID, your breathing stops and your mind races, making up horrible stories about what they will say when you answer . . .

Do this breathing awareness exercise often and notice how much easier it is to smile, drive, and speak on the phone, even with (former) breath-stealers. Use *this* page to note how well you do with practicing every hour. Also, write down any "aha's" or questions that come up around this exercise.

This one practice, done hourly, every day for a week will reset your stress–reaction and allow you to stay calm and focused. It's like a muscle that gets stronger the more you use it.

Yes, changing your life really is that simple, and that hard.

Your Path From Secret to Success

Now repeat the exercise and imagine that you are breathing in confidence with each breath. Remember to write about your experiences with this exercise here or in your notebook.

_____
_____
_____
_____
_____

Lesson 1: Day 2
– *RELAX* –

*It's not about you; there is nothing wrong with you.
It's about staying present.*

Applying the Lesson:

Take some time to reflect on the caveman's world. It was fraught with sudden dangers and yet he had a quiet mind when no danger or hunt was happening.

Use *this* page or your notebook to draw the "dangers & hunts" in your world. Your "dangers & hunts" can be any event, image, or thought that tenses you up. Surround each image with the words for what it connects to in your mind.

For example, an image of dirty dishes in the sink might be surrounded with sentences like: "He doesn't care that I worked all day," or "She's too lazy to clean up after herself and I'm not doing it anymore."

These thoughts reflect feeling frustrated, unloved, taken for granted, etc. . . This act of capturing the tense images of your life and the thoughts, and judgments that surround them will make it easier to shift them later. **DO THIS IN BLACK & WHITE, DO NOT USE COLOR ON THIS DRAWING.**

Your Path From Secret to Success

✓ Remember to breathe.

Lesson 1: Day 3
— *RELAX* —

It's not about you; there is nothing wrong with you. It's about staying present.

Applying the Lesson:

What would your day be like if you could be completely present with no thought of the past or the future? How might you respond to the events of this day if they had no meaning other than what is actually occurring?

Take some time today to practice staying present. Notice any thoughts that come up and record them here or in your notebook. *How does it feel to be present?* One great way to practice this is to go for a walk, keeping your mind focused on what is happening in front of your eyes, what your ears notice, and how the ground feels under your feet.

Staying "present" with other people around is more challenging. Remember to do your awareness/confidence breathing – it helps.

_____
_____
_____
_____
_____

- ✓ Remember to breathe.

Lesson 1: Day 4
– *RELAX* –

*It's not about you; there is nothing wrong with you.
It's about staying present.*

Applying the Lesson:

Are you remembering to practice confidence breathing?

Let's get real. This is a deceptively simple practice that many people resist and dismiss because the logical left brain cannot grasp how something so simple could help with the complex challenges of being in business today. The conscious practice of awareness/confidence breathing will not solve your problems. It will, however, allow your creative brain to be available to help <u>you</u> solve your problems.

Go back and re-read the instructions for the practice of awareness/confidence breathing, and practice now. Use the space below to write down any thoughts that come up while you're breathing in confidence.

What can you use to help you remember to practice breathing today? List your ideas and the places where a bit more confidence would be useful. Use this space or your notebook.

_____
_____
_____
_____

✓ Remember to breathe.

Lesson 1: Day 5

– *RELAX* –

It's not about you; there is nothing wrong with you. It's about staying present.

Applying the Lesson:

Have you noticed any odd thoughts coming up as you have practiced the breathing technique? Odd, meaning judgmental, argumentative, or funny? Write them here or in your notebook, they'll be useful later.

_____
_____
_____
_____
_____

Slowing yourself down to do this practice often brings up previously hidden resistance. This is awesome if you are aware of it and it is probably going to be in your way later if you are not.

Your Path From Secret to Success

Use this space below, or your notebook, to write down your thoughts around how this guide is structured so far.

_____
_____
_____
_____
_____

If the guide is working for you easily, "Great, I'm glad it is serving you!"

If it's a challenge, "Great, I'm glad it is serving you!"

✓ Remember to breathe.

Lesson 1: Day 6

— *RELAX* —

It's not about you, there is nothing wrong with you. It's about staying present.

Applying the Lesson:

Use *this* page, or your notebook to describe your favorite relaxing place.

Use the next page to draw your favorite relaxing place. This is a great time to start using colors in your drawings.

Describe your favorite relaxing place:

_____
_____
_____
_____
_____

✓ Remember to breathe.

Your Path From Secret to Success

Draw your favorite relaxing place:

Lesson 1: Day 7

– *RELAX* –

It's not about you; there is nothing wrong with you. It's about staying present.

Applying the Lesson:

Now you've had a lesson in retraining your brain and body to stay out of high alert. It will serve you if you continue to practice often. True confessions – when I forget to practice for a day, I notice. If I forget for two days, my team notices. If I forget for three days, my clients notice.

Commit to spend time imagining, or actually being in your favorite relaxing place once a day or more. Since the mind cannot tell the difference between being somewhere and imagining being somewhere, imagining being in your "relaxing place" will bring you into a more relaxed, calm state. It's only from a place of calm that lasting change can easily occur. Being able to stay calm will make every other lesson easier to experience and implement.

Use *this* page to write down as many pleasant, relaxing locations and experiences that you can remember. Fill up one of the "Notes" pages in the back if you need more space. This is a resource that will increase your ability to handle the challenges ahead, so fill it up – you cannot have too many.

_____
_____
_____
_____

Your Path From Secret to Success

✓ Remember to breathe.

Lesson 2:
– LISTEN –
It's All About "Them," Their "Mess," Their "Message," and Their "Why" – Except When It Isn't...

Relax! We're not talking about making real marketing or sales calls here.

When you are *thinking* about being on the phone, exploring getting booked for a speaking gig, or perhaps interviewing a prospective client, imagine making it **ALL** about them. This wasn't easy when I was struggling to make ends meet, that's why this is an "imagine" activity.

Back then, I wanted to make sure that the person I was talking to knew how smart I was and how much I could help them. Guess what I had to learn?

"No one cares how much you know until they know how much you care." — Theodore Roosevelt

Practice: Set a timer for 5 minutes.

Imagine being on the phone; willing to LISTEN long enough to learn about what's important to the person on the other end of the phone. If you notice yourself starting to feel rushed or impatient, go back to Lesson 1 and breathe until you can easily imagine yourself being able to smile as you LISTEN.

Your Path From Secret to Success

Write down your thoughts about putting this into practice. Don't worry. You'll have a framework to use before the real calls begin.

_____
_____
_____
_____
_____

Lesson 2: Day 1
– *LISTEN* –
Sometimes, it is about your mess.

Applying the Lesson:

When you LISTEN, you will want to be aware of where your own "mess, message, and why" connects with theirs.

This means you **MUST** know your own mess **BEFORE** you pick up the phone!

USE THIS SPACE, OR YOUR NOTEBOOK TO DRAW YOUR "MESS" IN BLACK & WHITE. DO NOT USE COLOR ON YOUR MESS (more on this later).

Your Path From Secret to Success

Think about the patterns of behavior that helped you adapt, cope, and survive in your "less-than-perfect" relationships. Get all the details into the picture that you can, right up to the moment where you built up enough energy to break the pattern.

- ✓ Remember to breathe.
- ✓ Write down any thoughts about your mess that come up today. Use the Notes Section in the back or your notebook to hold these thoughts.

Lesson 2: Day 2
– *LISTEN* –
Sometimes, it is about your mess.

Applying the Lesson:

Take time today to reflect on what it took for you to break the pattern of your "mess." *What broke your heart or pissed you off enough to make that change?* Write out your defining moments.

_____
_____
_____
_____
_____
_____
_____
_____
_____
_____
_____
_____
_____
_____
_____

- ✓ Remember to breathe.
- ✓ Imagine being on the phone, LISTENing.

Lesson 2: Day 3
– LISTEN –
Sometimes, it is about your mess.

Applying the Lesson:

Imagine being on the phone and curious enough to LISTEN until you can hear the similarities between their story and your own. Write down all the gentle questions you might ask them to get to that point. Include ways to learn what "need" they are having trouble meeting. What are they struggling with today?

_____
_____
_____
_____
_____
_____
_____
_____
_____
_____
_____
_____
_____

- ✓ Remember to breathe.
- ✓ Imagine being on the phone, LISTENing.

Lesson 2: Day 4
– *LISTEN* –
Sometimes, it is about your mess.

Applying the Lesson:

What was your new "pattern?" How did your life improve? Write down all the positive ways your life changed when you got tired enough of your "mess" to take a different action. This is the beginning of your "message."

_____
_____
_____
_____
_____
_____
_____
_____
_____
_____
_____
_____
_____
_____
_____
_____
_____

- ✓ Remember to breathe.
- ✓ Imagine being on the phone, LISTENing.

Lesson 2: Day 5
– *LISTEN* –
Sometimes, it is about your mess.

Applying the Lesson:

As you continue to spend 5 minutes each day imagining being in conversation with others, focusing on their needs and the similarities between your two stories – be aware that in a live conversation you will need to be alert to two things.

One: *Gathering their language.* Collect the precise words they use to describe their mess. Reserve or create a place, either on this page, on one of the extra pages in the back of the journal, in a separate notebook, or in a Microsoft Word document to write them down. (Note: the .doc is dicey; most people will clam up if there is a "device" in the middle of a conversation or if they hear keyboard noise.)

Two: *Stay alert!* It is possible to get so focused on gathering language that you lose track of the connection and end up only making "contact."

This is dangerous because, as any Electrician knows, "contact" can produce sparks and start fires! If you ever feel that you need to choose between gathering language and making a solid connection, choose the **connection** – every time.

Write down the language that you use to describe your own struggles and stuck places. Go ahead and get it down – just don't get attached to it! Their language may be different.

Your Path From Secret to Success

- ✓ Remember to breathe.
- ✓ Go ahead and imagine the words they might use.

Your Path From Secret to Success

Lesson 2: Day 6
– LISTEN –

Sometimes, it is about your mess.

Applying the Lesson:

Use this space to draw a scene of you completely connecting with the other person, caring enough about them that their "mess" is more important to you than your own. It is perfectly OK, in fact, it is critical, that here you use full color and fully express the emotion of a solid connection in your drawing.

- ✓ Remember to breathe.
- ✓ Imagine the best possible outcome.

Lesson 2: Day 7
— *LISTEN* —
Sometimes, it is about your mess.

Applying the Lesson:

Today we are wrapping up the practice of LISTENing.

Write out the conversation that you would like to have LISTENed to.

What caring questions would you like to be asked to help you open-up to getting the help you need?

Write them here or in your notebook.

_____
_____
_____
_____
_____

If, at the end of any conversation, or at the end of your caring questions, you ever realize that it is not you they need, be honest AND helpful. Use *this* page or your notebook to start your own personal "Who's Who" list of other helpful people, what problems they solve, and what outcomes they get for their clients. This is how you will build a network that will actually "work" for you!

Do not include anyone on this list just because you think you "should," it never turns out well.

Your Path From Secret to Success

My Who's Who?

_____
_____
_____
_____
_____
_____
_____
_____
_____
_____
_____
_____
_____
_____
_____
_____
_____
_____
_____
_____
_____
_____
_____
_____

- ✓ Remember to breathe.
- ✓ LISTEN to any thoughts that come up.

Lesson 3:
– SERVE –
It's About Helping Them HIRE You!

That's right; it is perfectly OK for you to learn how to help them hire you. By "hire," I mean, accept whatever you are offering. Speaking gigs, products, and clients are the same here. Learn the "Rules of the Game" that <u>your prospects</u> care about, know who's the final decision-maker, and always **be easy to work with**!

One way to be easy to work with is to be clear about what "need" you're best at filling for them, to give them a chance to get to know you, and to acknowledge and appreciate the time they spend talking with you. You will not have to "sell" them if they know that you deliver what they need, care about what's important to them, and are easy to work with.

Lesson 3: Day 1
– SERVE –
It's not about "proving my value" or "selling." It's about helping.

Applying the Lesson:

The first step to helping someone hire you is: Get really, really, clear on what "mess" or "need" you're best suited to solve for them. *As a Speaker, are you content or entertainment focused? As a provider, are you a physical pain-eraser, an emotional up-lifter, or a whole-life supporter kind of service?*

Write down all the **struggles, problems, and challenges** that you have ever successfully addressed for a client, a friend, or yourself. Use pages in the back of this journal or a separate notebook if you need more space ;-). Use your "language" list from the last lesson where you described your own "mess" to remind yourself of what struggles, problems, and challenges you've overcome successfully.

_____
_____
_____
_____
_____
_____
_____

✓ Remember to breathe, they need you more than you think.

Lesson 3: Day 2
– SERVE –

*It's not about "proving my value" or "selling."
It's about helping.*

Applying the Lesson:

Now write down, here or in your notebook, all the **benefits** that the people you have helped have gotten from having their "mess" successfully addressed. Again, use the language from your list. These words are the beginnings of your message, but we're not ready to put it together yet.

_____
_____
_____
_____
_____
_____
_____
_____
_____
_____
_____
_____
_____
_____
_____
_____

✓ Remember to breathe, you have more value to offer than you think.

Lesson 3: Day 3
– SERVE –
It's not about "proving my value" or "selling." It's about helping.

Applying the Lesson:

Now you get to play my favorite game! It's WSGAT time!
W.S.G.A.T. was taught to me by Bob Circosta of the Home Shopping Network. It stands for: "What's So Good About That?"

So, look at your "benefits" from yesterday. For each one, "WSGAT" it, meaning ask the question 5 times.

Ex.: If your client has reduced pain, a WSGAT of "reduced pain" 5 times looks like this:

   1. They can work longer.
   2. They have the energy to take care of themselves.
   3. They get to socialize.
   4. They can get on the floor with a kid or grandkid.
   5. They are happier.

As my messaging coach, Wendy Keilin says: "Try to make the outcomes as 'concrete' as possible." Tangible/touchable is good, sometimes not so easy. "Concrete" is better. Concrete simply means, easy to envision. For example, "work longer" is not tangible, but it is "concrete" for the person who hasn't been able to work much due to pain. See if you can make an even more "concrete" list. Again, use their language if you have it.

What have they said is important to them that they don't have yet? What's So Good About having That?:

1. _____
2. _____
3. _____
4. _____
5. _____

This exercise may take some extra time, so you may want to plan time this evening to complete it. We will use these outcomes shortly.

- ✓ Remember to breathe, this is time well spent.

Lesson 3: Day 4
– SERVE –

It's not about "proving my value" or "selling." It's about helping.

Applying the Lesson:

MORE of each? Yes! You can never have too many words that clearly depict the problems you solve, the benefits of solving them, and the **OUTCOMES** people get from having them solved.

If you're booking speaking gigs: The "Outcomes" might include: making the organizer look good. It is absolutely wonderful if the organizer gets lots of, or even all, of the glory for your positive reviews. *Why might that be?*

WSGAT that 5 times.
    1.
    2.
    3.
    4.
    5.

The goal is to get you to be seen as an expert and start making more money – however, if the thought of someone else getting the glory causes your body to tense up – use a page in the back or in your notebook for another B & W drawing of where you feel it. (You'll use this information later too).

    ✓ Remember to breathe.

Lesson 3: Day 5
– SERVE –

It's not about "proving my value" or "selling."
It's about helping.

Applying the Lesson:

Start putting the words from the last few days together into random sentences.

Take one Struggle, add one Benefit, and then two to three Outcomes. The more concrete the OUTCOME, the fewer you need.

It looks like this:

Struggle + Benefit = **Outcome, Outcome, Outcome**.

Ex. 1: I help people who are *struggling to make sales calls* get into consistent calling routines ***so that*** they have **more confidence and make more money.**

Notice the WSGAT answers go after the "***so that.***"

Ex. 2: "I help small business owners who *struggle with frustration and overwhelm,* permanently resolve the mental & emotional blocks that *hold them back and keep them playing small*, ***so that*** they can **stay calm, take risks, and make more money.**" There were two sets of "*struggles*" in this one.

Your Path From Secret to Success

Now it's your turn. Mix & Match – I'm giving you some extra space here to play – be adventurous – you may discover some true gems. This is a great game to play with a buddy.

_____
_____
_____
_____
_____
_____
_____
_____
_____
_____
_____
_____
_____
_____
_____
_____
_____
_____
_____
_____
_____
_____
_____
_____
_____

- ✓ Remember to breathe.
- ✓ They need you and you have more to offer than you know.

Lesson 3: Day 6
– SERVE –
It's not about "proving my value" or "selling." It's about helping.

Applying the Lesson:

Pick your best two sentences from yesterday. *Do any of them pull at your heart strings?* If not, you may want to revisit your "language lists" and mix and match a couple more.

Got two good ones?

This is where you get to draw again in both black & white and full color. This is a "bridge" moment – for each sentence, draw a picture with the struggle in black & white on one side and the outcomes in brilliant color on the other and a bridge in between. On the bridge, draw a picture of you and what you do.

There are extra blank pages at the back of the journal if you need more space for your drawings.

Note: In the back of this book or in your notebook, You may want to format this exercise (bridging) and similar ones on two adjacent blank pages, one even and one odd. The black and white can be done on the even page, the color on the odd page, and the *bridge* can easily be drawn between the two images.

Your Path From Secret to Success

Congratulations you just drew your sales conversation script! Wasn't that easy? ;-)

Draw another picture for the second sentence.

Your Path From Secret to Success

If you have more than two that you think really nail your message, draw another picture!

When you are done drawing, pick the two with the biggest emotional impact between the problem and the solution, and write them here.

_____
_____
_____
_____
_____

- ✓ Remember to breathe.
- ✓ They need you and you have more to offer than you know.

Lesson 3: Day 7
– SERVE –
It's not about "proving my value" or "selling."
It's about helping.

Applying the Lesson:

Find a willing friend (***NOT** a fellow "Guide User"). While you are with them or via Zoom/Skype, read your sentences to them one at the time. Notice by watching and LISTENing: *What impact does each sentence have on them?*

This was a humbling experience for me – I have a tendency to fall "in love" with my own writing. As difficult as it was, accepting feedback and shifting from my words into my client's language really improved my ability to connect and convert—so relish the feedback, positive or negative.

Remember, it's only feedback.

Rewrite your sentence until you think you've got it and then . . . find another friend. Yes, you may go through a bunch of friends doing this exercise – but that's better than burning through your network of prospects. Notice their feedback. Repeat until you have one sentence that seems to capture the pain/problem and benefit/outcome concepts in clear, concrete language.

Your Path From Secret to Success

Write your "one" sentence here.

_____
_____
_____
_____
_____

*Remember to get your friend's permission before you start! LOL, one time I forgot, and they thought I was hitting on them to become a client.

Next, we're going to put this all together.

✓ Remember to breathe.

Your Path From Secret to Success

Lesson 4
– ACT –
"Leap And The Net Will Appear*"... Eventually

It's time for action because the only way to get good at doing anything is to, well, do it! My intention is to guide you to do the right things in the right order so that you get comfortable with being in action sooner.

No one likes this part. It feels risky and you know you are going to get told "no" and you may even be afraid that you will "mess up" a few conversations. You will.

I told you, you are not going to like this. I get it. I didn't like it either.

The reason "Act" is Lesson 4 and not Lesson 1 is because I messed up a huge number of conversations getting into action before I had what I needed.

Mainly, I didn't have a single place to record what happened in the conversations, so it took me a very, very long time to notice patterns and to figure out how my "mess" connected to other people's messes.

Getting into action before I had the pieces, that you have been putting together in the earlier lessons, cost me time, money, and even a few relationships.

Your Path From Secret to Success

But because you have put in the pre-work, you'll have a much higher rate of successful conversations sooner. I know, that doesn't change the fact that getting into action feels not "fun" and risky.

The question I want you to ask: "Am I willing to be uncomfortable?" If the thought of getting into a conversation with a prospect still tenses you up – don't worry, it's just an "elephant" and we are going to tame it – one prospect at a time.

The script is simple.

If you are looking for customers and clients, or if you are looking to get booked for speaking gigs, the script is similar, and call lists begin the same way too. Starting with the easy part, each day of this lesson will build on the language lists you created in the last lesson.

Note: Just like Lesson 1 about breathing, this lesson will be an ongoing practice for the rest of your business life.

It may always be a challenge to get yourself to start moving on making calls; or you may find that it gets to be something you look forward to. Either way, for me, calls got to be fun when I started making money.

We worked through the language lists first because I know people will pay you to help them if you are addressing what is important to them, in language that sounds like what they say to themselves.

*American Naturalist, John Burroughs

Lesson 4: Day 1

– ACT –

*It's not about getting it right.
It's about getting it done.*

Applying the Lesson:

Get dressed in your business clothes and go to a networking event. No business cards? No problem.

If you've never been to a networking event or you simply don't like going to them, this plan will make it easier for you.

Your goal is to **LISTEN.**

Your goal is to collect contact information from 3 people that you want to have follow-up conversations with.

Your goal is to practice your "Problem/Solution" statement from Lesson 3 (the one that you tested out on your friends) with at least 10 people, 20 is better. Keep it verbatim – no changing it up yet.

Your goal is to leave with all of your own business cards still in your pocket.

HUH? Read that last line again – Do not, I repeat, do not, offer your card to anyone. Give them one if they ask for it, but otherwise, keep them in your pocket. Trust me, they do not need your card. In fact, sometimes it is an advantage not to have cards yet.

Now, take a deep breath. No one ever died from networking.

Your Path From Secret to Success

Here is one of my favorite ways to start a networking event. Look for a person on the edge of the room who is more nervous than you are (holding a folder in front of their stomach is a clue). Walk over near them and stand BESIDE them, not facing them. Glance at them, catch their eye, grin sheepishly, and say: "I'm not quite ready to jump into this yet, do you mind if I stand here with you for a bit?"

I have made life-long friends by asking this one question.

Now, go out and meet 3 people who might be good prospects for you. Write their names and phone numbers here.

1.

2.

3.

Use this space, or your notebook, to write down your experience networking this way

_____
_____
_____
_____
_____
_____
_____
_____
_____

✓ Remember to breathe.

Lesson 4: Day 2
– ACT –

*It's not about getting it right.
It's about getting it done.*

Applying the Lesson:

Following up is **THE critical activity** in business. Most people fail to follow-up enough to be successful because they haven't done the pre-work that you have. You understand that the connection is more important than the transaction. You have prospects from networking, business cards you've collected, and other people you know.

Write down a list in your notebook or start a spreadsheet. The columns you'll need are: Name, Phone number, Preferred Email, Notes, and Next Steps. Other columns will come up as you have conversations, but these will be enough to get you started.

Now call three, and only three, prospects.

Start every conversation with:

"Hi, this is (me) and we met at (event). Do you have a minute?" ("Yes.")

"I'd like to get to know you better and see if there are ways I can help you (Benefit Statement.) Would tomorrow morning at 10 work for us to chat for 30 minutes?"

The goal of these "reach out" calls is to set up a longer conversation. Pick a time in advance that you want them to schedule and be prepared to be flexible with it.

Your Path From Secret to Success

Note: *If you are in a network marketing/direct sales business, get with your mentor and plan your calling strategy. There may be a different call pattern that works in your industry. If your mentor has offered to do three-way calls with you to make it faster for you to grow your business, use them! Plan your calling schedule with your mentor AND change your script. Give your prospect the head's up that your mentor may be joining you on the call.*

For everyone: If your call goes to voicemail – hang up. Do not leave voicemail messages. I mean it. Do not leave a message. Let them be curious.

If an assistant offers to take a message, ask: "What's usually a good time to catch them?"

Now do your conscious breathing, smile, and dial.

Write your results here or in your notebook. It's important to track activity and results starting now.

All dials count in this game. Make notes in your notebook or on your spreadsheet and you're done. Whew.

Remember, it's all only feedback. *How many conversations did you schedule? How many dials did you make to get three people on the phone?*

_____
_____
_____
_____
_____
_____

- ✓ Remember to breathe
- ✓ Congratulate yourself for taking action.

Lesson 4: Day 3
– ACT –
*It's not about getting it right.
It's about getting it done.*

Applying the Lesson:

Having a conversation with a prospect is an opportunity to make a new friend. Let's review your preparedness for these conversations.

- **You have your relaxing picture from Lesson 1, Day 7.**
- **You have your gentle questions to help you learn what they might be struggling with from Lesson 2.**
- **You have your "Bridge" drawing to remind you that you are the connection that will get them from where they are to where they want to be.**
- **You have your "Problem/Solution" statement from Lesson 3 that you tested with friends and networking.**

You have everything you need except an invitation. You will need to invite people to work with you.

(Don't laugh, the number one reason people don't make money is that they do not <u>ASK</u> for it.)

What's your offer? What do you want people to do?

Buy your product? Join your team? Take a course/class? Hire you to speak? Become a client in a program? Have one free session at your gym? Join you at a meeting?

Your Path From Secret to Success

It depends on what you're ready to receive and what their needs are. Clarity will come from your conversations and from the later Lessons. You don't need to be clear yet. You simply need to make your calls and LISTEN.

Keep your conversation appointments.

At the end of the day review your imagined conversation from Lesson 2, Day 7 and compare it with your real calls. Write down what you learned from these calls. *What worked from your visualization? What didn't?*

_____
_____
_____
_____

Even though you may have conversation appointments today, you still need to make 3 more calls to prospects.

In fact, you will need to do this every day from this moment on. It will likely take you <u>10 dials</u> to get 3 people on the phone. Even if it's your second or third attempt to reach someone, do not leave a message yet. It will only slow you down.

- ✓ **Commit to making 10 DIALS every day. Do these before you do anything else, including checking email.**
- ✓ **Remember to breathe.**

Lesson 4: Day 4
– ACT –
It's not about getting it right.
It's about getting it done.

Applying the Lesson:

Start using tools to help you keep track of your dials and calls.

It could be a daily bubble chart with 10 circles that you can fill in for each dial. It might be a set of three circles for the names of your three conversation appointments, or a checklist. It could be a stack of poker chips that you move from one side of your desk to the other. Pick SOMETHING, it is vitally important that you have a visual way to keep track of your actions.

Use the space on this page and the next page to try out one of these ideas as you make your dials and calls today.

_____
_____
_____
_____
_____
_____
_____
_____
_____
_____
_____
_____

- ✓ Make 10 DIALS every day before you do anything else.
- ✓ Remember to breathe.

Lesson 4: Day 5

– ACT –

*It's not about getting it right.
It's about getting it done.*

Applying the Lesson:

Make your calls and then read this section.

Email contact has the same goal as the "quick call" and NO, email cannot be used in place of making "reach out" calls. The best way to use email is as a "reason" to call someone and ask: "Did you receive my email?"

How fast do you want success?

Nothing is faster than face to face contact for building connections.
Voice to voice contact is the next best option.
Email is slowest.

That being said, email is important and there are rules that make it more effective. Reach out emails are short, to the point, and most often used by speakers or to invite someone to something.

If you are looking for speaking gigs, your email might be simply:

"Do you take outside speakers for your meetings?"
(with a follow-up call to make sure that the email arrived to the correct person)

If you are looking for people to attend your event, your email might be:

"Please join me for my open house."
(with the Location, Day & Time – you'd be surprised at the number of invitations I receive without this information in the body of the email. Having the "where & when" only on the attachment is not as effective as making it easy for them to know if they can make it.)

These emails are not advertising or marketing messages, this is just about making solid contact so that you can call them and build connections.

Write down a list of when you might use an email to reach out.

_____
_____
_____
_____
_____
_____
_____
_____
_____
_____
_____
_____
_____
_____
_____
_____
_____
_____

Your Path From Secret to Success

Review the list, are any of the ideas just a way of postponing picking up the phone?

Keep the ones that will motivate you to reach out to people by phone faster and write them as a template in a Word document and save it where you can access it when you're writing emails.

- ✓ Recommit to making 10 DIALS every day before you do anything else.
- ✓ Remember to breathe.

Lesson 4: Day 6
– ACT –

*It's not about getting it right.
It's about getting it done.*

Applying the Lesson:

The Money is in the Follow-Up.

Repeat after me . . . "The Money is in the Follow-up!"

True story: I have a client who has many years of experience in business. She was constantly scared of not being able to grow and not being able to fund her normal life, much less fund her retirement. I suggested that she create a quick 1:1 consulting follow-up to the classes she was teaching as a fast path to create more income from current students.

Then I recommended that she call everyone who had ever taken this type of class in the past and make the offer to them as well. That's when I learned that even though she had kept files on every one of her clients, she had NEVER followed up with any of them . . .

. . . about anything.

Now we're doing a major remake of her business including adding amazing CUSTOMER SERVCE, a.k.a.: follow-up.

NOTE: Customer Service never goes out of style and if you get it right, it will set you apart in the marketplace.

I hereby challenge you to keep your commitment to do 10 dials-per-day to new prospects AND add 5 dials-per-day to existing and previous clients.

- ✓ Make your 10 + 5 DIALS every day before you do anything else.
- ✓ Remember to breathe.

Lesson 4: Day 7
– ACT –

*It's not about getting it right.
It's about getting it done.*

Applying the Lesson:

ACT - show up at networking events, follow-up with your prospects and clients and former clients. Remember to **LISTEN** and remember that it's all just **FEEDBACK** – it is not about you.

Check in – *What are you using to keep track of your outbound calls, call backs, and scheduled conversations? Is it working for you?* <u>This is important.</u>

Whatever you use, be consistent with it.

Earlier, I recommended setting up a spreadsheet to keep track of your calls. Here's why: Using a computer-based system makes it easier to scale your business. Spreadsheets will make it easier to delegate some of the phone calls to an assistant when you get to the point where it makes sense – like now?

If you are serious about building a business, planning when to hire an assistant is one of the first goals I recommend. Even 5 hours a month can take some of the busy work off your plate so that you can focus on making phone calls and having scheduled conversations. Plan what to delegate before you start looking for help. At an early stage, you cannot delegate reach out calls or emails.

You need the feedback.
- ✓ Make your 10 + 5 DIALS every day before you do anything else.
- ✓ Remember to breathe.

Lesson 5:
– CREATE –
You Only Get One Story In This Lifetime... The One That You Create.

Other people's opinions and beliefs can limit your income and happiness. Most of the time, we have "Other People" in our heads. Their beliefs about how the world works were absorbed by us through our skin when we were young.

When we're young, we don't have filters and whatever we see, hear, and experience starts building up a body of evidence that will control every aspect of our life – as long as we are unaware of it. These belief systems act like a <u>cruise control</u> without an "off" switch—a cruise control that we weren't given the instruction manual for. Until now.

This is where the rubber really meets the road and you might decide to take what you have learned so far and stop right here.

If you do, you'll make more contacts, create better connections, and make more money – for a while.

Then your limiting belief systems will kick in the cruise control and you'll stop following-up, and stop making calls every day, and your income will decrease. I'm sure you've seen it happen, and in the past, this hasn't been your fault because you were operating with an invisible, pre-programmed, limiting belief based "cruise-control" running in the background. It was truly an "Elephant in the Room."

Are you ready to acknowledge it?

Your Path From Secret to Success

If you choose to keep working through the course, you will gain control over your ability to create the life you want. This includes making and keeping more money, making and keeping more joy, and making and keeping more loving relationships.

Sound good? Let's get to it. Truth: We all have a past.

Observation: Many people believe their past is the "reason" for their present and the predictor of their future. They let their past define and limit them.

What I've learned working with 100s of clients is that our past can be our greatest asset once we learn to use it as raw material for building our dreams. Our past is made up of more than just events, it's made up of the thoughts and feelings we have around those events and the beliefs we created from those thoughts and feelings, a.k.a.: the meanings we assigned to those events and events that are similar to them.

When I look back at how long I stayed married to a man that I did not love, and how long I stayed married to a man that I was afraid of, it's a wonder that I didn't stay stuck even longer! I used to relive all the emotional mess and think that I wasn't smart enough to help others because I was barely smart enough to help to myself.

Then I got it! If I could help myself at all, I could help those who couldn't do that yet.

Warning: There's something about being willing to help where I was comfortable that made it both easy to get started and easy to stay broke.

The lesson I had to learn: Success comes at the cost of comfort.

Creating your own story will not be comfortable, it will involve risk, AND I guarantee you, it will be worth it.

Lesson 5: Day 1
– CREATE –
It's not about having a "story."
It's about not letting the fear of being judged for it, make it the only story that you live.

Applying the Lesson:

Everything you see, hear, and experience adds to the programming. Reprogramming requires being very mindful of what you are exposing yourself to, avoiding what could be reinforcing what you don't want, and consciously choosing to be exposed to the people, thoughts, and emotions that will make you stronger.

Other than this book, what are you reading?

If you haven't read Dale Carnegie's: **How to Win Friends and Influence People**, I highly recommend it. In fact, even if you've read it before, if you haven't read it this year, I recommend that you read it again!

Use *this* page to create a list of the inspiring books you have read and the ones you want to read.

Inspiring Books I Want to Read (or Re-read!)

_____
_____
_____
_____
_____
_____

Your Path From Secret to Success

Make a commitment to read one of them for 10 – 30 minutes every day. No excuses. If you don't have a book in your current space – go, get a library card or look up the free library online and download one of the classics. Reading or LISTENing to inspiring stories is one of the foundations of change because you have to come to believe that success is possible before your mind will allow you to consistently take new actions and produce new results.

- ✓ Make 10 + 5 DIALS every day before you do anything else.
- ✓ Remember to breathe.

Lesson 5: Day 2
— CREATE —
It's not about having a "story."
It's about not letting the fear of being judged for it, make it the only story that you live.

Applying the Lesson:

CREATE your own inspiring story.

Start by answering the following questions. Just jot the answers down on this page, or in your notebook.

1.) Where have you stood up for yourself?
2.) What were you afraid of?
3.) What was the outcome?
4.) What happened, in that moment, that you were willing to stand your ground?
5.) When have you ever NOT taken "NO" for an answer?

Now, answer them again. Keep writing – create a body of evidence that proves that you can stand your ground, that you can act, even in the face of fear or other people's limiting opinions.

Feeling a little more confident? Feel free to keep writing.
_____
_____
_____

Your Path From Secret to Success

Start your day with re-reading what you wrote here. Remembering that it's possible for you to stand your ground and break a pattern will help you learn how to help other people believe that it's possible for them to stand their ground, be a little more confident, and act, even in the face of fear or other people's limiting opinions.

- ✓ Make 10 + 5 DIALS every day before you do anything else. People need your help.
- ✓ Remember to breathe.

Lesson 5: Day 3
– CREATE –
It's not about having a "story."
It's about not letting the fear of being judged for it, make it the only story that you live.

Applying the Lesson:

Keep writing about the times in your life where you stopped running, stopped hiding, stopped being "stoic" and "handling it."

This is a great time to draw your hero self. Use full color. Use the pages in the back of the book or your notebook.

_____
_____
_____
_____
_____
_____
_____
_____
_____
_____
_____
_____
_____
_____
_____
_____

- ✓ Make 10 + 5 DIALS every day before you do anything else.
- ✓ Remember to breathe.

Lesson 5: Day 4
– CREATE –
It's not about having a "story."
It's about not letting the fear of being judged for it, make it the only story that you live.

Applying the Lesson:

As you build up your body of evidence and begin to see yourself as the hero in your own story, other people in your life will try to save you from success.

It's true. In all love, they will help you stay small because being successful is scary. They have their own pre-programmed success cruise control and it will kick in on your behalf.

You need to plan how to handle their "help" with grace. Love them and greet any signs of discomfort as validation that you are growing. When they tell you that you "will never make it," or, "no one will pay you for that," BREATHE. Allow them to have their say, and then respond with a "one-liner."

A one-liner is just that, one sentence that you will deliver in a completely calm manner. Mine is: "You might be right."

It's from the assertiveness training book: **When I Say No, I Feel Guilty** by Manuel J. Smith (which, by the way, is another good book to add to your reading list).

Use *this* page to write a list of who you might need to have a plan for. A plan for how to deal with their "help." Be honest with yourself. There is no blame in someone being on your list. It's simply an acknowledgement that your growth is outside of their current comfort zone. With time, they will adapt – or not.

Until you write your own one-liner, feel free to borrow mine. Practice it in front of a mirror until you can say it in a calm, even tone.

So, who's on your list? Whose help slows you down? Write down their names and make a one-liner plan.

_____
_____
_____
_____
_____
_____
_____
_____
_____
_____
_____
_____
_____
_____
_____
_____
_____
_____
_____
_____
_____
_____
_____
_____
_____
_____
_____

- ✓ Make 10 + 5 DIALS every day before you do anything else.
- ✓ Remember to breathe.

Lesson 5: Day 5
– CREATE –
It's not about having a "story."
It's about not letting the fear of being judged for it, make it the only story that you live.

Applying the Lesson:

What do you plan to do with your increased income? Today you get to write down the pieces of your dream. A dream is the basis of all change. *What will you change in your life once you accept that you are capable of creating and sustaining more income?*

List the thoughts that just came up here or in your notebook:

_____
_____
_____
_____
_____
_____
_____
_____
_____
_____
_____
_____
_____
_____
_____

- ✓ Make 10 + 5 DIALS every day before you do anything else.
- ✓ Remember to breathe.

Lesson 5: Day 6
– CREATE –
*It's not about having a "story."
It's about not letting the fear of being judged for it, make it the only story that you live.*

Applying the Lesson:

You are about to activate your imagination. Using your imagination will keep your cruise control on the sidelines, for the moment anyway.

Two blank pages follow so that you can do the exercise here or use your journal.

On the left blank page, **Before Achieving Your Dreams:**
sketch in black & white all the things in your life right now that are not the way you want them or are just "OK." Stick people and bare outlines are fine.

On the right blank page, **After Achieving Your Dreams:**
draw in living, vibrant colors the way your life looks when you have achieved your dreams. Draw the house you will live in, the awesome cowboy boots you will wear, the great team you will have helping you build your business, all the good things from yesterday's list. Fill this in with great accents and make it look as compelling as you can.

When you're done, look over your "before" page. *What can you add to make it even less happy?* In the "Draw Your Future" TEDx Talk* *they drew an image of a face blowing out cold winds or maybe you need one spitting angry words at you . . .*

Your Path From Secret to Success

Once you have a significant gap between your current state factors and future happiness factors, draw three arrows from the left side bridging over to the right side. On each arrow write one action you can take that will move you towards your future.

Note: This is similar to the bridging exercise in Lesson 3 Day 6

* From 2015 TEDx Talk: "Draw Your Future" by Patti Dobrowolski.

Before Achieving Your Dreams:

After Achieving Your Dreams:

- ✓ Make 10 + 5 DIALS every day before you do anything else.
- ✓ Remember to breathe.

Lesson 5: Day 7
– CREATE –
It's not about having a "story."
It's about not letting the fear of being judged for it, make it the only story that you live.

Applying the Lesson:

You have now created your "inspiring story" from your past. You've created your plan to deal with the less than inspiring people in your present, including your own thoughts (by reading every day), and you've created your plan for your life with more money and better relationships in it.

The biggest challenge we have is when we pretend that something is what it isn't.

My present is not perfect. It is a heck of a lot better than my past, but it is not perfect, and I never expect it to be. I do expect it to get more and more fun as I learn to create better ideas faster.

And "faster" looks like having the idea to write a book and one month later having it written, and in my hands – including finding an editor! This is not bragging, it's simply proof that it can be done.

If I can create my life, learn to ask, and not be afraid to share my "stuff" with the world, with all the baggage I used to carry, anyone can do it!

Let's put it all together by filling in the blanks:

I use my past to _____ my present, so that I can _____ my future.

My take on the fill-in-the-blanks:

When you can use your past to **ACCEPT** your present, without shame, guilt, or the need to blame anyone for it, then and only then can you use your past to easily **CREATE** your future.

List here, or in your notebook, all the other inspiring word combinations that you could use to fill in the blanks. Then write the best ones on index cards or Post-It notes and put them where you can see them and read them every day to inspire yourself.

_____
_____
_____
_____
_____

- ✓ Make 10 + 5 DIALS every day before you do anything else.
- ✓ Remember to breathe.

Your Path From Secret to Success

Lesson 6:
– SHARE –
It's The Best Way to Help Them

You are in business, doing what you are doing, to help other people, right? You might be helping them grow their business, improve their health, level-up their golf game, build better teams, fit into skinny jeans, grieve their pets, or grow more hair. No matter what form your help takes, to help them, you must have the willingness to share yourself with them. And, they deserve everything that you can offer.

Mostly, they need to trust you. They need to learn that you have a depth of experience and a depth of knowledge. When you can share both of those freely and confidently, you will be easy to get to: **Know, Like and Trust.** Once they know, like, and trust you, they will let you help them and they will willingly, even gladly pay for that help.

Lesson 6: Day 1

– SHARE –

*It's not about being seen as perfect.
It's about being seen as real and relatable.*

Applying the Lesson:

Check in with your "depth of experience." You absolutely must have a depth of experience, either your own or your clients, to share from. Write down the experiences that have given you the best insights into what works and what doesn't – in your business and in your life. Write down what you learned from all the things that did and didn't work. Use simple, short sentences.

If you question whether or not you have enough experience, go back to Days 2 and 3 in Lesson 5 and "create" more.

Fill this page with notes about your experience and use pages in the back or in your notebook for more space.

_____
_____
_____
_____
_____
_____
_____
_____
_____
_____

- ✓ Make 10 + 5 DIALS every day before you do anything else.
- ✓ Remember to breathe.

Lesson 6: Day 2

– SHARE –

**It's not about being seen as perfect.
It's about being seen as real and relatable.**

You'll be well served to add to your list of experiences every day. After all, you do have experiences every day, don't you? If you spend two minutes every night jotting down your experiences of the day, you will amass a fantastic body of evidence to share from very quickly.

Collecting your experiences and analyzing them for the lessons you learned from them, will make it easier for you to view yourself as competent and qualified. This viewpoint will make you even more attractive to your tribe.

Take a minute and write down what you've experienced so far today.

_____
_____
_____
_____
_____
_____
_____
_____
_____
_____
_____
_____
_____

- ✓ Make 10 + 5 DIALS every day before you do anything else.
- ✓ Remember to breathe.

Lesson 6: Day 3
– SHARE –

**It's not about being seen as perfect.
It's about being seen as real and relatable.**

Applying the Lesson:

Now, check in with your "depth of knowledge." The sooner you get to seeing yourself as an "expert," the easier it will be for you to invite people to work with you and for them to say "yes."

How do you know that you have an "expert" level of knowledge?

Count up how many books you have read on your subject matter.

Write the number of books on your topic here: _____

Depending on your field, there may be a number of professional (peer-reviewed) articles on your subject.

Do you know of at least one? How many have you read in the last year?

Write the number of peer-reviewed articles here: _____

If the total of those two numbers is less than 100, it is time to up your game.

No matter how much experience you have, the easiest way to get more and better clients, and speaking gigs is to offer more value. This means you need to add to your storehouse of knowledge by reading (studying with a mentor counts **_only if_** they are globally recognizable in your field).

Your Path From Secret to Success

It's also possible to offer more value by interviewing those who have knowledge you don't and sharing the interviews with your tribe.

(Note: "tribe" to me means a group of like-minded people who enjoy learning from and with each other. Feel free to substitute any word that fits for your worldview.)

Start a list of people, here or in your notebook, who have expertise that you know would be a valuable add-on to your work.

_____
_____
_____
_____
_____
_____
_____
_____
_____
_____
_____
_____
_____
_____
_____
_____
_____
_____
_____
_____
_____
_____
_____
_____
_____

- ✓ Make 10 + 5 DIALS every day before you do anything else.
- ✓ Remember to breathe.

Lesson 6: Day 4
– SHARE –
**It's not about being seen as perfect.
It's about being seen as real and relatable.**

Applying the Lesson:

Getting the reading done.

Just like having a practice of making your calls and measuring your results, practicing your breathing, and capturing your experiences; reading every day will help you move toward your goals.

I use a "5x5 Morning Practice" to help myself stay grounded and get my reading done.

The 5x5 is a daily practice designed to help you accomplish your reading and life goals in a faster, more consistent way. This is especially useful if you know that one of your challenges is keeping commitments to yourself. There are 5 different 5-minute activities. Hence the name.

You'll need a timer for timing 5-minute increments, an inspirational book, a notebook and writing implement, and a quiet place where you will have uninterrupted time, for 30 minutes.

Today – pick your book. Go to the library if you need to. I like business inspiration and personal development books for this. I started with the classics, like Dale Carnegie's, **How to Win Friends and Influence People**, Denis Waitley's, **Seeds of Greatness** and Jack Canfield's, **Success Principles**.

If you're part of our online community, please post the book that you are using for the 5x5. Perhaps your book will inspire others. If you're not, venture over to: https://www.facebook.com/groups/SellingWithConfidence/ and join the "tribe."

- ✓ Make 10 + 5 DIALS every day before you do anything else.
- ✓ Remember to breathe.

Lesson 6: Day 5
– SHARE –

**It's not about being seen as perfect.
It's about being seen as real and relatable.**

Applying the Lesson:

Here's how the 5x5 works.

1. The first 5 is "Read." Set the timer for 5 minutes, pick up your book, and read.

2. When the timer goes off, put down your book, reset the timer for 5 minutes, pick up the notebook, and "Write." For 5 minutes, write about what you just read. What made sense, what questions came up, whatever comes to your mind will be the right thing to write down.

3. When the timer goes off, put down your notebook, reset the timer for 5 minutes, close your eyes, and "Reflect." Reflect on what you just read and what you just wrote. Just give yourself time to let the information sink in.

4. When the timer goes off, reset the timer for 5 minutes, pick up your notebook. This 5 is for "Receive." Receiving is about expressing gratitude to yourself for everything that is good in your life at this moment. And—I do mean everything that is good in your life. Pick something in your life that you are happy about and receive gratitude to yourself for the fact that it's in your life because of the choices that you've made. You brought this into your life yourself, it can only be there because you made choices that brought it to you. You took those actions. This is important. For 5 minutes, receive gratitude for the choices you have made that brought good things into your life.

5. When the timer goes off, set your timer again, and in this last section "Re-engage." For 5 minutes, noodle out how will you apply what you read, wrote, and reflected on. *How can you apply it in your life?* Now, if there's something that you can apply immediately, turn off the timer, and just go do it! You're no longer constrained by 5 minutes here, if you can get it done, go get it done! Sometimes, just noodling it through is a great use of 5 minutes.

Ask and Answer the following questions either here or in your notebook:

"How might the information and insights change my conversations?"

"How might that impact a relationship?"

"Who do I want to practice this with?"

When the timer goes off this time, put away your notebook, your book, your timer, and your pen. Keep them together in one place so that you have them together the next morning.

That's the other 5 minutes, that's why I said the whole practice takes 30 minutes, because you need a couple minutes to set up and a couple minutes to pack up. Setup & pack up, "bookending" your practice makes it easier to continue it the next day.

Now, please take a few minutes and answer the question:

"When I think about committing to a daily practice, I feel...?"

_____
_____
_____
_____

- ✓ Make 10 + 5 DIALS every day before you do anything else.
- ✓ Remember to breathe.
- ✓ AND make space on your calendar for the 5x5 – commit to doing it every day for 30 days.

Lesson 6: Day 6
– SHARE –
**It's not about being seen as perfect.
It's about being seen as real and relatable.**

Applying the Lesson:

What aspect of your primary business are you most interested in, at this moment? Is anyone writing about it online?

Read online articles until you find one that you respond strongly to. Write and post a response expressing the impact of the article/book and your opinion, either pro or con.

Use *this* page to draft a response to a provocative article.

Not finding an article? Ask your tribe to share with you articles that they think relate to you. Responses can be written or you can post short video responses.

Getting article suggestions will also help you learn what your tribe thinks you do. This is very useful for honing your message. Remember, it's all just feedback.

This was another of those humbling moments for me. Quite a few people thought I worked only with chronic pain sufferers. All I could do was pick my jaw up off the ground.

Yes, reducing stress can certainly reduce pain and promote the body's natural ability to heal, and yes, I'm on a mission to get <u>pain-reducing socks*</u> on the feet of 1,000 job-challenged veterans this year, but pain relief is certainly not the only outcome of the work my clients do with me.

Most of my clients are interested in improving their bottom-line by making more sales! Visibility and cash flow first, everything else, including mental and emotional healing, is a bonus!

In that moment, I had to remember: "It's ALL Feedback" and feedback is very useful for helping us move forward. Something to keep in mind as you test your message and interact with your tribe.

- ✓ Make 10 + 5 DIALS every day before you do anything else.
- ✓ Remember to breathe.
- ✓ Complete the 5x5 every day for 30 days.

* www.SocksForHealth.com

Lesson 6: Day 7
– SHARE –

**It's not about being seen as perfect.
It's about being seen as real and relatable.**

Applying the Lesson:

We're going to start this lesson with a Visioning Exercise.

Visioning Exercise

Take a deep breath. And again.

Repeat until you remember to pause before the release.

Slowly fill your lungs with air, pause, and then release the air even more slowly.

Breathe in again.

Notice the air flowing into your body.

Notice the way your body releases the air effortlessly.

Now notice the movement of your mind, as you consciously breathe in, not just air, but confidence.

And breathe out, releasing anything that is not that.

Breathe in again – imagine that you're filling your mind with confidence.

Now breathe out, releasing anything that is not that.

Imagine the air flowing over you, as well as flowing inside you.

Both one and the same, within and without. Breathe.

Your Perfect Day

Now, imagine your perfect day. Imagine waking up, refreshed and eager to start the day. Each breath opens you up to enjoying this vision of your perfect day a little more. *What are you reading? What are you tasting? What view are you enjoying as you complete your morning practice and begin your day?*

Imagine having interesting people to call and engage with. Imagine creating amazing partnerships and enjoying the challenges of bringing more value into the world through your business.

Write down what you "saw/heard/felt" as you envisioned your perfect day.

_____
_____
_____
_____
_____
_____
_____
_____
_____
_____
_____
_____

- ✓ Make 10 + 5 DIALS every day before you do anything else.
- ✓ Remember to breathe.
- ✓ Complete the 5x5 every day for 30 days.

Your Path From Secret to Success

Lesson 7:
– ACHIEVE –
Growth Is Continuous.

Imagine the joy! You've arrived! You're recognized as a Speaker. You've been handed a check – before you even open your mouth— from a group that "doesn't pay speakers!"

You've earned over $10,000 in a single month and that's becoming a trend...

You've got it figured out, right?

I thought I did – but I didn't.

Here is a real "elephant in the room" story. We don't ever "arrive" or get it "figured out."

You might argue with me over this one, I don't mind. I stand my ground – if you're in business, you do not ever get to stop growing and adapting. The alternative is to shrink and go back to being invisible.

Just look around you. Which businesses have stopped innovating and not started descending into invisibility?

Avoiding that trap sound good?

Rereading this book will help.

Here's why: "ACHIEVE" means that you're never done. The only way to help your clients/audiences grow and improve is if you continue to grow and improve. The goal of this lesson is to keep you growing.

Lesson 7: Day 1
– ACHIEVE –

**It's not about arriving.
It's about growing.**

Achieve – Measure – Repeat

Applying the Lesson:

"Consistency helps."

This is where all the notes you took earlier will be helpful.

Making and keeping micro-commitments will keep you growing.

Theorists and experts have written tons of books on this topic, so we will not explore the why and how of goals and goal-setting here.

Here's what was important about it to me. Keeping micro-commitments to ourselves is what allows us to see ourselves as trustworthy. When we see ourselves as trustworthy, we attract trustworthy people into our world.

There are a lot of additional benefits from doing the practices and activities in this course and at the risk of repeating myself: *"Consistency helps."*

Use the rest of this page to list the practices and activities from the earlier lessons that you have attempted, implemented or plan to implement.

Your Path From Secret to Success

Practices:
Confidence Breathing

LISTENing

Visualizing Conversations

Saying Your "One-Liner"

Activities:
Attending Networking Events

Gathering Words

5x5 Morning Practice

Drawing Goals in Color

You get the idea – go back through the book and list the rest of them here or in your notebook.

_____
_____
_____
_____
_____
_____
_____
_____
_____
_____
_____
_____
_____
_____
_____
_____
_____
_____
_____

- ✓ Make 10 + 5 DIALS every day before you do anything else. (*Did this one make it on your list?*)
- ✓ Remember to breathe.
- ✓ Complete the 5x5 every day for 30 days

Lesson 7: Day 2
– ACHIEVE –

It's not about arriving.
It's about growing.

Achieve – Measure – Repeat

Applying the Lesson:

Read over the list from yesterday.

Which activities were easy to implement on a consistent or a "more-often-than-not" basis?

_____
_____
_____

Construct a tracking chart, some way to measure your activities. Earlier, I recommended that you use tools to keep track of your daily reach out calls. This might be a bubble chart, a spreadsheet, a stack of poker chips . . .

For tracking your overall practices and activities, I suggest a simple spreadsheet and then plotting the numbers on a wall graph. Put a big piece of paper on a wall with simple numbers up the left side and time written as "Day 1, Day 2" across the bottom. Use different colored lines for each practice or activity.

At the end of each day, give yourself a point for each activity that you completed. Then, plot your points on the wall chart. The goal is to measure effort and action in a visual way.

Your Path From Secret to Success

The more you can increase your level of awareness around the choices you make and the actions you take, the faster you will experience having control over your time.

Use this idea or create your own visual tracking method. You can draft a small chart here or in your notebook, and then make a big chart for your wall.

Note: a hand-drawn chart is more flexible that a spreadsheet (see example below).

Reachout calls
Customer Care calls
Morning 5x5

Activity					
10					
9					
8					
7					
6					
5					
4					
3					
2					
1					
	Day 1	Day 2	Day 3	Day 4	Day 5

Hang it where you can see it every day. Kids use their bedroom walls. Helping kids learn to measure their efforts and activities, as well as their accomplishments, will give them a leg up in life (and they think it's fun!).

Your Path From Secret to Success

- ✓ Check and update your chart.
- ✓ Remember to breathe.
- ✓ Complete the 5x5 every day.
- ✓ Make 10 + 5 DIALS every day before you do anything else.

Lesson 7: Day 3
– ACHIEVE –

It's not about arriving.
It's about growing.

Achieve – Measure – Repeat

Applying the Lesson:

There is a lot in this course. Repetition will be required to master any single lesson.

You'll notice that at the bottom of each page in the journal we've been creating and adding to a checklist of my "Core 4" activities and practices: "Check and Update Your Chart," "Confidence Breathing," "5x5 Morning Practice," and "Make Your Calls."

If you have worked through all the activities, in order, then these will form a bedrock for your growth.

Create your schedule: *When in your day will you do each one of the Core 4?*

Right now, get out your calendar and schedule them on each day for the next week. On Sundays, review your week and revise your schedule of the Core 4 activities. Commit to these four and your business will grow.

Are you willing to commit to each activity? Which one is the easiest? Which one is the most challenging?

Your Path From Secret to Success

Write your answers here or in your notebook and if you're not ready to commit yet, write down what's in the way.

_____
_____
_____
_____
_____
_____
_____
_____
_____
_____
_____
_____
_____
_____
_____
_____
_____
_____
_____
_____
_____
_____
_____
_____
_____

- ✓ Check your chart.
- ✓ Remember to breathe.
- ✓ Complete the 5x5 every day.
- ✓ Make 10 + 5 DIALS every day before you do anything else.

Lesson 7: Day 4
– ACHIEVE –
It's not about arriving.
It's about growing.

Achieve – Measure – Repeat

Applying the Lesson:

In your connection calls, what problems are people talking about?

Review your "ideal conversations" and "language lists."

Are your prospects and clients talking about the problems on your original list?

Now that you have had multiple conversations, which of the problems are costing your prospects and clients the most, in terms of time, dollars, and sleepless nights?

Write them down here or in your notebook.

What are their top three? What is the dollar cost to them for not fixing them? Are you able to help them with 1 or 2 of these?

1.

2.

3.

Your Path From Secret to Success

Which ones are your strong suit? How much is it worth for your clients to fix these? Be brave and honest when you assign numbers. How big is the problem they are struggling with that you can help them solve?

Reconnecting with this information will help you place value on the services and solutions that you provide.

And remember, the one mental trigger that positions you as the "go-to expert" the fastest is your ability to explain the pain of your customer exactly the way that they do . . .

_____
_____
_____
_____
_____

- ✓ Check your chart.
- ✓ Remember to breathe.
- ✓ Complete the 5x5 every day.
- ✓ Make 10 + 5 DIALS every day before you do anything else.

Lesson 7: Day 5
– ACHIEVE –
It's not about arriving.
It's about growing.

Achieve – Measure – Repeat

Applying the Lesson:

Are you still using the introduction you created in Lesson 3?

If you have stayed with the same introduction statement, you have amazing focus and you must have nailed it!

For the rest of us:

Write your current introduction here and the original one below it. Review the problems you listed yesterday.

_____
_____
_____
_____
_____

What language can you pull from the problems list and add to your introduction?

_____
_____
_____

Your Path From Secret to Success

Remember: Use one version of your introduction, without changing it, at least 20 times. This "20-test" will help ensure that you have enough feedback before you tweak the words. (Unless it falls completely flat – a.k.a., your friends tell you it is confusing.)

Revisit Lesson 3, Day 6 and then draw a new "bridge" picture on the next two blank pages, or in your notebook.

Ready to Draw?

- ✓ Check your chart.
- ✓ Remember to breathe.
- ✓ Complete the 5x5 every day.
- ✓ Make 10 + 5 DIALS every day before you do anything else.

Before Achieving Your Dreams:

After Achieving Your Dreams:

Lesson 7: Day 6
– ACHIEVE –

It's not about arriving.
It's about growing.

Achieve – Measure – Repeat

Applying the Lesson:

The easiest way to make more money is to bring more value.

Knowing what problems you can solve is valuable; increasing your ability to solve them quickly makes you even more valuable in the marketplace. This is about adding to your "Depths of Experience and Knowledge."

Want the fastest path to having more of both?

Buy someone else's!

BREATHE - This is completely acceptable. In fact, purchasing the rights to use someone else's knowledge and experience is the most common form of explosive business growth.

Licensing and franchise operations are good examples.
(Here you thought that there was something "wrong" with using someone else's knowledge.)

Write down as many other examples of where someone else's depths of knowledge and experience could be "bought" and used to bring more value to your clients.

Your Path From Secret to Success

✓ Check your chart.
✓ Remember to breathe.
✓ Complete the 5x5 every day.
✓ Make 10 + 5 DIALS every day before you do anything else.

Lesson 7: Day 7
– ACHIEVE –

It's not about arriving.
It's about growing.

Achieve – Measure – Repeat

Applying the Lesson:

Bring more value, make more money.

Everything you have studied, pondered, created, and worked through in this course has been designed to clear some mental clutter, focus your attention and actions, and raise your awareness of your value.

The commitments you make and keep, the practices and activities you chose to repeat, will determine your future. **NOTHING ELSE DOES.**

You may have started out thinking that the lessons would be simple—they were.

The lessons were simple and possibly confusing at times. That was completely intentional.

Now, I know that a confused mind cannot make a decision, so I try to never confuse a prospect.

My clients on the other hand, sometimes my clients need to have their paradigms challenged so they can shift them, and a bit of confusion sometimes helps with that.

Your Path From Secret to Success

You may have started out thinking that you would find the secret to success, you did.

The secret to success was revealed early on, it just wasn't labeled. The Secret to Success is understanding that:

It's not about validating other people's opinions of you. It's about being self-aware enough to validate your own.

This Guide is simply a place to get started.

Reuse it often.

And. . .

REMEMBER:

- ✓ **Check your chart.**
- ✓ **Remember to breathe.**
- ✓ **Complete the 5x5 every day.**
- ✓ **Make 10 + 5 DIALS every day before you do anything else.**
- ✓ **Randomly working the Lessons will give random results at best. Let us help you stay on track.
Join the Online Community for more support:
https://www.facebook.com/groups/SellingWithConfidence/**

Important Points to Ponder and Accept:

- I will be confused, and the speed of change will only increase.

- Some people are not going to like me. The sooner I accept this; the less power other people will have over me.

- Failure will be required. Change is not possible without it.

- Networking and Speaking are about showing up for the one person who is "hanging off a cliff." Whose life could I save by showing up and throwing them a rope?

- Clarity increases your value. The lack of clarity around why someone would want to work with you is reflected in the number of people who say "No" to your offer.

- **Take ACTION** – Nothing else will get you what you want in life – **_nothing_**.

- AND here is the final "Elephant in the Room."

This is the cure for a major limiting belief – ready???

YOU DO NOT
HAVE TO BE PERFECT
TO BE *PROFITABLE*!

About the Author

Removing the "Cloak of Invisibility" from her business skyrocketed Jackie Simmons from Secret to Success in 7 Months. But it didn't start out that way.

Did you know that there's nothing like being an entrepreneur/business owner to stir up an emotional mess?!?!

For Jackie, being a single mom at the same time brought her smack up against mental and emotional blocks that shut her down each time she was making progress —like an unacknowledged "Elephant in the Room."

An "Elephant" that sat on her phone so she couldn't make sales calls, and distracted her so she couldn't focus and finish projects. An Elephant that trashed her hard work and stunk up her relationships.

It was through learning to permanently "tame" the Elephant that the Ultimate Sales Mastery Course was born. Jackie used the course to help herself, and then her clients, become calm, focused, and profitable.

You can learn more, grab a Success Journey Roadmap (Jackie's Gift to you) and connect with Jackie at www.SuccessJourneyAcademy.com

Notes:

Your Path From Secret to Success

Your Path From Secret to Success

Your Path From Secret to Success

Your Path From Secret to Success

Your Path From Secret to Success

www.ingramcontent.com/pod-product-compliance
Lightning Source LLC
Chambersburg PA
CBHW060808050426
42449CB00008B/1592